BUSI

SUCCESS

How To Write A

Business Plan

Peter Oliver

HOW TO WRITE A BUSINESS PLAN

Copyright © 2016 by Concise Reads™

CONCISE READS™

Concise Reads was created to distill complex material into small morsels of knowledge that can be readily consumed by today's busy reader. At its core, Concise Reads is a living breathing brand that focuses on feeding knowledge to our always hungry entrepreneurial spirits. This knowledge is exactly what we wanted to learn but without having to pay thousands of dollars in fees for formal courses.

How much knowledge and how little time you spend to understand it, *together*, define value. We hope you enjoy the concise bits of value in the Concise Reads books, and we hope to continue to create more titles with time.

TABLE OF

CONTENTS

INTRODUCTION

A business plan is a document that outlines in detail what the business is and how it will generate revenue. It is a projected roadmap to success that typically takes into account the next 1-5 years of the business lifecycle. A business plan is often referred to as a 'living document', meaning that it is not set in stone but rather evolves with new information or new circumstances as the business grows. Venture capitalists and general investors in a business like to see a business plan so they can gauge its potential for success.

It is important to note that generally any estimate of costs or revenues projected into the future are likely to prove inaccurate with time, but that doesn't make them any less important. When an investor evaluates your projections, they are evaluating whether you have thought of the future and accurately accounted for it given the best information available at the time. In the same token, it helps the small business owner prepare for future costs or hurdles ahead of time.

While the generally accepted format may seem somewhat rigid, it is intended for others reading your business plan to follow a logical thought process and possibly skim through to the sections they deem most valuable. Some sections may require more in-depth analysis depending on the type of business you are creating, and that will be evident to you as you read through this book and begin this process.

The most important section is the executive summary since that is the first section investors read. Pay attention to sell your business here rather than summarize your business plan. Although counter intuitive, this section is written last— only after you've done all your research can you really make a pitch as to why investors should invest in your business.

The last section of this book explains the elements of a slide deck, which is the digital presentation (PowerPoint or PDF format) used to pitch your company to investors for funding. It is essentially the executive summary in slide format. The 'ask' or funding request section is easily omitted when repurposing the slide deck for presentation to a general audience, and repurposed as a pricing slide when used for sales meetings.

In terms of formatting, make sure to use a Sans-Serif font such as Arial in digital documents as it is easier on the eyes, or a Serif font such as Times New Roman in printed documents with the headings in Sans Serif.

Serif is a Dutch word for *line* and describes the hard lines at the end of letterings while *Sans* is a French word that means *without.*

The business plan should have 1 inch margins, 12pt font or larger, numbered pages, justified text, and consistent headings. Some ask if it is appropriate to add pictures to the business plan, and that is absolutely fine as long as they are used to stress a point and included in the appendix. Keep the body of the business plan image/figure/table free. If you plan to print and send your business plan, then add a cover page with your company name, logo, and contact information. To go the extra mile, use professional binding to hold the document together.

EXECUTIVE SUMMARY

The executive summary is the most important section of your business plan. Do not be fooled into thinking there is a requisite minimum length. It is as long or as short as it takes to summarize your business plan and sell it. Having said that, the executive summary can range anywhere from a single page to several pages.

The executive summary follows the same section format as the business plan. The difference is that you start with a <u>mission statement</u>. To sell this section you need to focus on your strengths and downplay the weaknesses.

If you are a startup with very little traction, then you'll make sure to sell the qualifications of the founders. If you have an amazing product but an inexperienced team, then focus on the product and its market potential. Similarly, if you are an established company with prior success, then make sure to stress your track record.

The following are the typical sections of a business plan (+appendix) and the executive summary (+mission statement and summary):

A. Mission Statement
B. Company Description
C. Market Analysis
D. Management
E. Service or Product
F. Marketing or Sales
G. Financial Projections & Funding Request
H. Summary
I. Appendix

MISSION
STATEMENT

This section shouldn't be retrospective. This is why you founded the business to begin with. It is the purpose of the business and its guiding principle. It doesn't need to be more than a paragraph long but it should not sound like a simple goal, rather it should sound like a call to arms for anyone who agrees with the statement. So make sure most people would agree with it.

In that sense, it can be as broad as Google's mission statement:

"to organize the world's information and make it universally accessible and useful"

A clever and appealing statement like Warby Parker's mission for their affordable eyewear business:

"Warby Parker was founded with a rebellious spirit and a lofty objective: to offer designer eyewear at a revolutionary price, while leading the way for socially-conscious business"

Or even a longer format, in what is known as a mission *narrative,* that still briefly explains a company's vision, values, and strategy. Sometimes a tagged shorter slogan is included that can be used on product labeling. Ben & Jerry's 'Vermont's Finest' cleverly included all their stakeholders, or entities that come into contact with their business, into their mission statement and then proceeded to explain their set of values:

"Ben & Jerry's operates on a three-part mission that aims to create linked prosperity for everyone that's connected to our business: suppliers, employees, farmers, franchisees, customers, and neighbors alike.

Product Mission: To make, distribute and sell the finest quality all natural ice cream and euphoric concoctions with a continued commitment to incorporating wholesome, natural ingredients and promoting business practices that respect the Earth and the Environment.

Economic Mission: To operate the Company on a sustainable financial basis of profitable growth, increasing value for our stakeholders and expanding opportunities for development and career growth for our employees.

Social Mission: To operate the company in a way that actively recognizes the central role that business plays in society by initiating innovative ways to improve the quality of life locally, nationally and internationally."

COMPANY DESCRIPTION

The company description is very similar to the mission statement but expands on it. The mission statement summarizes the **why** of the company, and the company description details the **what**.

A good approach to this section is to:

1) Briefly explain the type of business: For example: PieArt, LLC is a Bronx based pizzeria)

2) Summarize the problem: Unlike Brooklyn, the Bronx suffers from a lack of artisan pizzas and delivery costs limit adoption of Brooklyn based products.

Pizza sales in the Bronx alone account for as much $150 million in annual sales.

3) Describe your product(s) or service: PieArt, LLC provides masterfully created artisan pies with locally sourced ingredients in the popular framework of 'farm to table'. The pies are produced in a piccole (8"), medie (12"), and grandi (16") sizes varying in prices (cost) from $6 ($4.15) to $18 ($12.80).

4) Describe your competitive advantage (talent, intellectual property, efficient processes, lower costs, etc): Led by Chef Jean Poupart and his internationally trained artisan staff, PieArt, LLC produces unique creations that are difficult to mimic in taste or design, and each artisan pizza is priced similar to non-artisan pies. These cost savings are made possible because PieArt, LLC was created

as a vertically integrated extension of the existing PieArt Farms that produces the majority of ingredients used.

The Company description is a good opportunity, if you haven't already done so, to evaluate and put to paper some of the more intangible facets of your business principles, ideals, and cultural philosophies that will allow you to better grasp your own corporate identity.

The Company description can differ in format or length because every business is different in some way (or should be if you are applying for funding).

One thing to *stress* for this section: Sometimes, and this is a knee-jerk reaction, when a differentiating factor is lacking in a company description, entrepreneurs hope to stress the expertise of the team. Although it is important to sell yourself, and I am a big believer in that, it should not stand out as the only competitive advantage your business has to offer. If that is the case, then be more thorough with your market analysis and see if your product or service has a differentiating factor.

Economists believe the US is mainly made up of incompletely monopolistic markets where there are many sellers with slightly different products. In business school, marketing courses gain followers when the teachers begin to explain how similar toothpaste or shampoo bottles are but how people actually believe there is enough of a difference to pay completely different prices. We'll cover marketing your business in another concise read in this series but I hope you understand that every sales pitch begins with how you or your product is different in some shape or form.

MARKET ANALYSIS

This chapter usually elicits a sense of frustration and fear just thinking of the work involved to have a great market analysis. First, it is not difficult and should not be frustrating. There is a whole field of marketing consultants paid thousands of dollars just to write this simple section or present their findings in PowerPoint format to company executives. There have been books written on this, and professors who devote their life teaching the principles of Market Analysis. In the end, even though it has the word 'analysis' in it because you spent a few hours doing research, it is by no means a quantitative unpublished statistical analysis. As you become a more established entrepreneur you will notice terms like 'analysis' or 'science' pop-up for content that is observed and recorded which technically qualifies as science, but usually only involves searching online or searching through company sales data.

To demystify, let's start with understanding what a market is. A **market economy** is one where free will and preferences dictate the demand and supply of any particular good. On the other hand, a **centrally planned economy** is one where a government intervenes so much that prices, demand, and/or supply can be fixed. In this market economy, there are hundreds of thousands of different markets. The term market simply defines characteristics or attributes of the exchange of some product or service between a buyer (demand) and seller (supply).

I can use the term "housing market" and the reader would understand I am referring to the market where houses are bought and sold. I can be more specific and use the term "Austin housing market". Once I understand what market I am selling my product in, then I can begin to describe all its attributes and characteristics (market analysis) with the goal of showing that there is an **opportunity** (competitive analysis) in the market for my product to make a profit.

The market analysis sets the scene. Think of it as consisting of two parts. Typically, we start by describing the market and then describe how our product fits in this market.

We'll want to describe a number of both general and specific demographic characteristics that apply. This can be as detailed as is necessary. Some of the questions asked are:

- Where do they live?
- What's their age range?
- What's their level of education?
- How many of them are there?

- What are some common behavior patterns?

Let's use an abridged example of four paramedic friends and a wealthy investor colleague who want to open their very own nationwide ambulance service called <u>FastTransfers, Inc</u>:

1. **Industry**: Emergency Ambulance services.

Sometimes what's known as an *Industry Cost Structure* is included here, and is important when writing a marketing plan (an expanded version of our market analysis typically created by marketing management or hired consultants). However, in this case, we leave any cost 'analysis' in the financial section.

2. **Market size, growth rate, & expected trend:** $48 billion spent on emergency medical services, of which $6 billion were spent on ambulance services. In fact, spending on ambulance services has increased more than 300% in the past 10 years alone and is expected to continue to increase with the aging of the baby boomer population.

3. **Stakeholder Analysis** (who is involved, their values, and the advantages and challenges of adopting your product): Patients, Providers, and Payors (Medicare/Medicaid/ Insurance companies) would be the correct stakeholders for FastTransfers, Inc.

The *competitive analysis* section has the sole purpose of showing the market opportunity. To complicate matters (or to simplify them for some people), marketing professionals use the STP analysis which stands for market Segment, Target Population, and Product Positioning. Let's see how this is applied with our four friends and the wealthy investor colleague:

A. **Segment**: 140 million Americans visit the emergency room annually with 15-20% of them arriving by ambulance.

B. **Target Population**: The majority of patients are non-critical but are incapacitated in some way and require ambulance transfer including the elderly, nursing facility, psychiatric, and special needs patients.

C. **Positioning**: In terms of contracted ambulance transfer, FastTransfers faces minimal competition in the discount sub-market, and in the direct to consumer contract sub-market. It faces tough competition with already established contracts in large hospitals, and psychiatric facilities.

Positioning can sometimes be drawn as a visual map if there are few significant competitors in order to demonstrate what aspects your business is competing on for the same market of buyers or consumers. For example, this can be a simple X-Y axis with cost on the X-axis and quality or complexity on the Y axis.

Next in the competitive analysis section is to describe who the competition is. This can be as simple as describing the 2-3 firms with the largest market share. Alternatively, there are two different ways to describe the competition in the market and some use both methods, but being verbose can either win you points for being thorough or lose you points for being unfocused. Learn from Goldilocks or Buddha and find the right length in the middle. The popular formats are:

(1) **SWOT analysis**: There are four factors to consider in this section:

Strengths	Weaknesses
Opportunities	Threats

This table can be any shape you prefer or even 4 paragraphs. This somewhat objective, but mostly subjective section is best written by someone who understands the business. In this case, as the founder, just draw a 2x2 table, sit down with a refreshing drink of your choice and start writing. The point of the SWOT analysis is to give you (and your investors) more information with which to build your marketing strategy.

(2) **Porter's 5 Forces**: This is an analysis named after Michael Eugene Porter, an Economist at Harvard Business School. Its purpose is to determine how profitable your business is likely to become and maintain profitability by looking at **internal** factors that can affect your business. The point is to know if the business is in such a competitive market

that it would be very difficult to make a profit or if there is some inefficiency in the market to allow for a profit to be made. These 5 forces can be answered in short free-form text or in bullet points. They are:

a. **Supplier Power**: how dependent you are to the supplier and hence how much the supplier has in terms of changing prices, quality or other expected attribute depends on how many other suppliers exist who can do the same job and how costly it is to switch.

b. **Buyer Power:** Similar to supplier power, how many buyers are there and how costly it is to acquire a new buyer will determine the buyer's power in determining the price and the additional services that you will offer.

Express Scripts ended its contract less than 2 years since signing with startup PillPack, a mail-order online pharmacy. That cost PillPack a third of its business, making it a very hard, but not impossible, pill to swallow for the young startup.

c. **Competitive Rivalry:** What is the scale of the competition, 1-2 competitors, or 100? Is the competition based on price, location, or some other factor? Is the market large enough to accommodate you or will your entry cause increased competition from existing firms?

d. **Threat of Substitution:** Are there other products or services similar to what you offer that consumers can substitute to. What would make this more or less likely?

e. **Threat of New Entry:** Are the barriers to entry such that any competitor can enter the market? Are the profits so attractive that a large company with a similar or related product or service could simply use its resources and expand into your market?

(3) **PESTEL analysis:** This is another 'analysis' that takes into consideration the **external** factors that can affect your business. This looks into the **P**olitical, **E**conomic, **S**ocial, **T**echnological, **E**nvironmental, and **L**egal factors. This

sort of analysis is more commonly seen in business plans of larger companies or business that depend on regulation and/or external factors like mining for raw materials, multi-national enterprise, etc. For the sake of brevity, this is not important for a startup unless there is a strong external factor that should be mentioned such FDA regulation for a small biotech or the effects of exchange/inflation/interest rates for a fintech startup. Just to be clear, this section similar to the other sections should consist of only a few bullet points or short free-form text for each topic considered.

(4) **STEEPLE:** identical to PESTEL with the addition of the **E**thical factor which identifies social values for the business

and/or the community the business operates in.

ORGANIZATION & MANAGEMENT

This is a very simple section and varies in length depending on how many employees or advisors are involved and how simple or complicated the company organization is. As a general rule, simple is better than complex and visuals beat written explanations. The most common question for this section is how much information to provide. The simple answer is to provide as much information as possible. Most will only look at the diagram of the company structure and the payscale strategy. In this section, it is encouraged to sell the investor on the management team. The typical format for this section is as follows:

1) **Structure of Organization:** A simple flowchart is the best representation. This is easy to do using PowerPoint SmartArt under 'Hierarchy'.

2) **Executive Management & Divisional Descriptions**: All business plans should explain the structure of the business (Proprietorship, Partnership, Incorporated, etc), details of ownership stake, and descriptions of the management team. The description of the management teams are short 1-3 paragraphs describing attributes such as position, education, past experience, past successes, awards or recognition, community involvement, and/or hobbies/interests. Believe it or not, most successful entrepreneurs and executive management started by understanding

what a business plan was and how to write/read one. As they began to see success in business or in corporate life, they sat down at some point and wrote a short blurb of who they were and what their strengths were. They then kept that short summary with them and modified it a little with time. Interestingly, on a company's website you will see a short blurb usually in 3rd person describing the CEO of the company. If you look up that same CEO on linked-in or read an article about them in the news, you will see that the same information is either copied verbatim or slightly paraphrased. In this case, you don't need to re-invent the wheel. If the management team has not created their first blurb, they should start now along with a professional picture that can bc used for any future news articles or social media. Lastly, for larger companies who are updating their business plans, it is important to describe the function and scope of the major divisions, whom they are led by, and any successes or challenges the division has faced in recent months. This can be broken up into small paragraphs for each division.

3) **Advisory Board and/or Business Partnerships:** This section is optional. Many technical firms have an advisory board of leading domestic and international experts. Since the business plan is not only a guideline but also a marketing and sales document to attract investors, you should describe every board member using that same professional blurb which they more than likely have already established. In addition

to describing the board members, you should note if they will be paid or not, how they will be paid (shares, deferred salary, etc) and how they will likely contribute to the future success of the company. This last part is important and it may show up in questions from the investors. Thinking of how the advisors will play a role in the future success of your company is _required strategic thinking_. If you plan to move your children's product from online and retail sales to Disney merchandising for example, then imagine how strategic it is to have a member on the Board of Disney on your advisory board? In other words, it makes no sense to have family members on your advisory board unless it's strategic, and it does make sense to have family members on your board of directors if your strategy is greater control of your company. This section is important to describe any partnerships that your business has established. Partnerships come in many forms whether it is two businesses profiting from a partnership (ex: Bose speakers in all Mercedes vehicles) or important in the supply chain that leads to your final product (ex: Manufacturing and assembly of the Apple iPhone in large Chinese factories such as Pegatron or Foxconn).

There are many tools to create flowchart diagrams. Find something that is easy because this part should only take you a few minutes. Powerpoint or MS word are easy. If you are working in a group, you can use google drawings for free. For a more professional service you can use a subscription service like Gliffy, Lovely Charts, Creately, etc.. (so many cloud based services!). However, there is no need to pay for simple flowcharts. Once your company grows, there are more powerful software solutions like Adobe suite and Sketch that have multiple other useful features.

PRODUCT OR SERVICE DESCRIPTION

Fortunately, this section requires very little external research unlike the market analysis section. This section describes in detail your service or product. If you have multiple products, then describe each one in detail making sure to group very similar products where you can to improve the readability of this section. The typical information expected per product or service are as follows:

A. **Description:** what is the product or service? what are the components that make it up? What is it used for?

B. **Developmental Stage or Product Life Cycle:** Sometimes the product or service you have is not the final version or iteration you have envisioned. In this case it is important to describe what stage you are in and where you expect to be as the next logical step. For example, you could have a prototype and the next stage would be a pilot study or launch in a specific community. You could also expect additional research and development or a period of user testing before commercialization. Alternatively, you could have a commercial service that is only licensed to operate in three states with expected regulatory approval for 6 more states in the next 3 months. This information is important because it helps describe what the final product or service is that investors will expect a return on their investment from.

C. **Competitive advantage:** A new company could have many things going for it but usually there are 1-2 attributes that really define the company. These can come in any form from special relationships (like the story of monopolistic Ma Bell and decades of favorable government regulations), or special cost advantages (like Harry's razor blades which cost half as much as those of the larger competitors), or a more robust advantage in the form of patented intellectual property (like the fingerprint sensor button that can only be used in Apple products).

MARKETING AND SALES MANAGEMENT

Earlier we talked about marketing analysis which described the market, outlined the internal and external forces facing your business, and compared your product or service to what is offered in the market by highlighting your competitive advantage.

That was a lot of useful information. In this section you tackle your marketing and sales strategy, sometimes shortened to marketing strategy or go-to-market strategy.

To get started, we first define our **marketing mix**, which is a business tool to help come up with the right marketing campaign for your product. A marketing campaign is not limited to print and television ads. It can take any form from social media to community involvement as long as the story or message is consistent and will (indirectly) generate more sales.

The marketing mix was first described by Michigan State Professor E. Jerome McCarthy in 1960. The first iteration had 4 Ps:

1. **Product**: What is the product? Use an adjective to explain its attractiveness factor. (Ex: artisan pizza, on-demand ambulance service)
2. **Price**: What is the price and where does that fit in the market. For example, although Harry's razors are described as German engineered quality razors, they are in fact 'discount' razors in terms of price.
3. **Promotion**: How is the product currently or planned to be promoted?

4. **Place**: Where does the customer have to go to buy your product or service? Is it convenient?

A few decades later, an additional 3 Ps were introduced to bring our alliteration to 7 Ps in order for an entrepreneur to assess whether their product is ready to be marketed and what the message will be.

1. **Physical Evidence**: This describes the form/shape of your proof of concept. Does your product have a trial service? Is it already in millions of homes? Does it have thousands of positive reviews online?

Having physical evidence is important. It is what investors call **traction**. Nobody wants to be the first one to buy a product or service, hence the success and proliferation of so many blogs, review services, and even for-hire book reviewers. On a personal side note, we try to keep our book reviews 'organic' and haven't paid anyone.

2. **People**: This describes who is selling your product or who is the face of your company. This section would be a competitive advantage for places like Hooters, the Titled Kilt, Apple genius bar, Geek Squad, and The Honest Company.

3. **Process**: This is an interesting recent addition to the P mix. As the science of business expanded over the past few decades, things like 'supply chain' and 'distribution channels' or the input and subsequent output process of your

product/or service became important. So important in decreasing costs and increasing sales that entire books and courses are devoted to them. The Process can be explained with a few lines of text highlighting the major pathways in bringing your product or service to the customer from A to Z or using a simple flowchart using familiar power-point tools.

As a side note, and although not important for the initial business plan, it is important for a budding entrepreneur to know that **LEAN** manufacturing and **six sigma** are business 'analysis' tools used to come up with ways to decrease costs, and increases *sales* through decreased *waste* and *variation* which in turn improve *speed* and *accuracy* respectively. Today, these two have merged into what is known as 'lean six sigma'. More on *Processes* and operation management will be covered in an upcoming Concise Reads.

For recreational reading, The Toyota Way by Jeffrey K. Liker and LEAN SIX SIGMA pocket toolbook by Michael L. George et al are recommended reading in operations management.

Once the 7Ps are defined, next is to explain your strategy in a short narrative or a series of temporal or sequential steps. There is no perfect way to format this section but It can be divided as follows:

Marketing Strategy: First define the market penetration for your product. Penetration, although an odd word choice, refers to how much of the market has your product been made available in. If the market has 100 grocery stores and you have it in 10 stores, then that is a 10% penetration. If there are 100 million patients with diabetes who can use your medication, but only 10 million patients use it, that is a 10% penetration. Having established that there is *room to grow*, so to speak, then you explain how you will reach as close to 100% penetration as you can. Then importantly, you define the following:

1. **Mission Statement/Vision/Tagline:** This is the message you want to communicate to the public. Granted you already defined a mission statement in your executive summary (not in the business plan), here is where you can expand on that a little bit more.

A world famous slogan whose evolution could fill books was L'Oreal's "Because I'm worth It" which was first introduced in 1971 to launch its hair-color business. The reason it was so powerful was because the brand message was capitalizing on the already growing movement of female empowerment and independence.

It's amazing how a consumer product would have any meaning whatsoever except to make money. That is how powerful a strong vision or mission statement can be to frame your brand.

More recently, social entrepreneurship has captured the hearts *and* wallets of consumers. The reason it works is because consumers don't want to give their money away but if they have to, giving it to a company that helps others and makes a profit is better than a company that just makes profit. This is especially true for the same quality product.

If you sell socks and promise to donate a pair of socks to the homeless then not only are you making a profit with increased demand, but you are also warming up the feet of a grateful homeless person. The government with so much money doesn't even have a decent sock donation program for the homeless. Maybe they do, but are they anti-microbial with a reinforced seam? Bombas socks is apparently using this marketing strategy to increase demand for its product which sells for about $12 (or a discount of 5% if you buy 4 pairs).

2. **Communication Strategy:**

Networking events, direct marketing (sales letters, brochures, flyers, cold calling), advertising (print, online, or television), blogging, trade shows, or through social media (twitter, Facebook business page, popular forums). There are multiple ways to get your message across.

Sales Strategy: This is sometimes known as a sales forecast. First it shows a breakdown of sales (current or potential) by pre-specified segments. Remember the earlier Segmentation, Target, and Positioning (STP) described in Market analysis? Here you break down sales by that segment whether it is geographic (New York vs. Los Angeles), age group (Millennials vs. Baby Boomers) or any other demographic that works in your industry.

After breaking down the sales landscape, then you specify a measure that is important for sales growth. This metric can be as simple as sales per quarter growth of 30% across all the smaller markets where your product is sold. After you define your goal and your metric then you begin listing the sales strategy which differs between companies only because business models are not fixed. Some people come up with interesting sales strategy. Some examples include:

- *Distribution strategy:* a lot of companies use a commission-compensated sales force to lower employee costs but also to incentivize employees or contractors to go out there and sell, sell, sell! Alternatively, a company can wholesale to regional distributors, or skip the sales force team and sell entirely through a third party like Amazon.com.

- *Pricing Strategy:* In the original market analysis we described where we are priced or where our quality lies relative to the rest of the competitors in the market. Here you decide if there is anything you can do about your position to improve it such as coming up with a better pricing strategy.

Many Authors for example sell the first book in their series at a discount to hook as many readers as possible. Shows like QVC and HSN hold off on showing you the affordable high quality add-on product that you can't live without until they've sold you the first product. That way your brain thinks 'since I already have the main product, and it is so reasonably priced, might as well buy it to have the complete set'.

Together the marketing and sales strategy give a go-to-market action plan if you've never been to market. After you've sold your first unit and have thus 'arrived' at the market, then you should just use the words marketing and sales growth strategy.

FINANCIAL PROJECTIONS

The financial section of a business plan is a pretty straightforward set of three statements, the balance sheet, the Income statement, and the statement of cashflows. This last one, the statement of cashflows, will have additional columns showing a projection of revenue and variable costs over an arbitrary number of years, typically 1-5 years. These projections are almost never accurate, but what investors and anyone considering offering you a loan is interested in is the methodology behind how you came up with these projections.

Saying that your revenue is going to increase 50% year after year just because you expect people to like your product will clearly prove that you haven't thought about the future cash flow. The easiest way for an investor to know that you made up the growth rates for both revenue and cost is if these numbers are fixed (i.e. 50% or even a conservative 10% every single year without change). So how do you come up with a relatively fair estimate of cash flows? Simple.

You look at your growth rate for the past few years and add that to the industry growth rate to get a % growth per year in revenue. Then you look at your costs and find out at which production levels does total cost decrease because the more you produce the lower the cost that you expect. Then subtract that discount from the total % growth of cost.

We use those percentages for the next 3 years to come up with informed projections for your cash flow. Again, these projections are completely made up based on the best information available. Every investor knows that. Next, Let's take a look and define what the three accounting statements are.

1. **Income Statement:** This is as simple as listing revenue and expenses and then subtracting one from the other to get net income. This is also known as a Profit & Loss or P&L statement.

2. **Balance Sheet:** This lists all assets whose sum is equal to all liabilities and owner's or shareholder's or stockholder's equity. Assets are anything the company owns including buildings, land, accounts recievables (from clients) and even liquid cash. Liabilies are anything owed and includes owed salaries, accounts payable (ex: to suppliers), interest on a loan, taxes, and wages. Owner's equity is typically the difference between what is owned and

what is owed. So if a $100 company owes $30 then it is actually worth $70. If this owner's equity is divided by shareholders then it can further be divided into common or preferred stock, and retained earnings.

Retained earnings is the net-income from the income statement that was not used to pay liabilities or buy assets and is considered free cash waiting to be used for something in the future. For a fun exercise, take a look at Apple's 10K (its annual financial statements) to see how much cash they have as retained earnings.

3. **Cashflow Statement:** This breaks down the changes in the balance sheet and income statement into three categories, operating, investing, and financing

activities with a final line showing what the net cashflow is *in a given year*. The breakdown is based on weather money is coming into the business or leaving it. Cash flow looks at the changes of the income statement and balance sheet because that is the liquid money being exchanged.

The three statements can be presented as three tables with a short free-form text description. Make sure to explain or highlight any abnormalities like a recent short-term loan with an above average interest rate.

REVENUE
————
EXPENSES

ASSETS
LIABILITIES
+ OWNER'S EQUITY

CASH IN
————
CASH OUT

Lastly, if accounting is not one of your strengths you have two options. Hire an accountant or read the Concise Reads book on accounting principles.

FUNDING REQUEST

When it comes to a funding request, what you are really doing is assigning a valuation to your company and asking others to believe in your valuation. Some entrepreneurs actually have no idea how to value their company and just ask for the amount needed to reach the next milestone. If you are a medical device company, then investors would much rather have you tell them how much you need to reach each milestone (prototype fabrication vs. pilot study vs. 510K submission) and then derive a valuation from there. However, if you have proven traction, such as a letter of intent from buyers then that will shoot up your valuation.

The value of a product is exactly what someone else is willing to pay given the means to do so. Twitter, Uber, Square, Tesla, and multiple other companies were valued in the billions, without significant profits at one point. Theranos raised over $600 million since being founded in 2003. Of course we all know what happened there.

The point is that these valuations can be overpriced, but as long as the investor is not the last one holding the bag, they can profit from the exchange. Having said that, there are 3 traditional ways to value a company: by estimating the value based on its (1) **Assets**, (2) **Future Income**, or (3) **Market comparisons**. Because Assets are only valuable during liquidation or sale of all company assets for their present cash value, we will look at the DCF method which uses future income to come up with a valuation for a business and comparable transactions and multiples methods which use other similar companies in the market to come up with a valuation. Again, if accounting is not one of your strengths, try your best to read this section, but definitely hire someone or pickup another Concise Reads to build your knowledge.

A. **Discounted cash flow (DCF) analysis**: The free cash flows are projected to infinity (typically 20 years or so) and then a net present value of these cash flows is estimated. *Free* because it is cash from earnings after taxes and capital expenditures are paid. If we assume your free cash flow (FCF) next year is $100 then the present value of that in *today's* dollars is $100/(1+\text{interest rate})$. This gives a smaller number which makes sense since $95 dollars today has the same purchasing power as $100 next year. You do that for n years or $100/(1+\text{interest})^n$ and sum all the present values to arrive at a net present value or NPV. The interest rate used is what is known as a discount factor (because you discount the future value). This discount factor can be calculated in different way, the most common is what is called a WACC or weighted average cost of capital method. This is what investment banks and larger venture capitalist firms use in growth stage companies rather than earlier seed stage companies only because they have positive free cash flows.

The Quick DCF: if you're not into using excel or estimating cash flows for the next 20-30 years then there is a crude but extremely fast method. If we assume cash flow is the same year after year, then we just divide the first year's free cash flow by the interest rate of a long-term treasury bill (T-bill) or 1/interest rate. This gives us the value of buying a T-bill that pays our free cash flow year after year.

B. **Comparable transactions method**: This method simply looks at the valuation of another similar company in a similar transaction (ex: merger, or straight buy-out) received while taking into account some metric like the company's earnings, or revenue. This is similar to homebuyers and real estate agents discussing *'Market Comps'* or market comparables for prices of similar homes in the neighborhood.

C. **Multiples method:** Very similar to comparable transactions, except you base the valuation as a multiple of a metric for the industry and not for a specific company. For public companies, the Price to Earnings ratio (P/E ratio) is often used. Technology companies often have valuations that are several, often as high as a hundred times, multiple of their Price to Earnings ratio. That's not the case with financial companies. But that's why when you combine finance with technology and call it *fin-tech*, you get the higher technology valuations. Some argue that Square which handles credit card processing should not be considered a technology company and should be valued at the P/E of finance companies. Other financial companies are trying to promote the idea that they are a technology company. For a lot of brick and mortar businesses, the typical valuation floating around is 5 times the sales or 10 times the profit. These are extremely rough estimates.

APPENDIX

The Appendix is where every figure, table, or image is included. Even though it may seem clearer to include them in the section of the business plan where they are mentioned, you shouldn't. In a formal business plan, the body of your text is kept clear, concise, and well organized. This means that your appendix is well organized as well. Every figure and table needs an ordinal position (Ex. Figure 1, Table 1, etc..) and a title explaining what one is looking at it.

For figures that require you to stress a point such as a growth trend in the double digits compared to competitors, make sure to clearly state that in the title and again in the short description! <u>Always assume that readers skim</u>. It is a poorly understood phenomenon, but intelligent and not so intelligent folks skim just the same. Writing has thus changed to accommodate those readers, and that is a good point to keep in mind when writing titles.

The appendix to a business plan sometimes includes the following list of items that are optional but help showcase your company:

- Logo & marketing material including advertisements.
- Recent company related news articles or headlines
- Highlighted resumes (founders, recent C-suite hire, or board of advisors)
- Front page of signed contracts with suppliers/distributors such as a large purchase order

Having hopefully cemented this concept of keeping the body of the text separate from the associated figures, tables, and images, it is important to note that the Appendix serves a different purpose in a PowerPoint presentation. The general rule of thumb is to have as little text as possible and use powerful figures, tables, and images to get your point across. All other figures, tables, or images that you did not directly talk about but will likely answer a question from the audience with are placed in the PowerPoint appendix. These do not need an ordinal numbering system.

Some people end up printing the appendix prior to a PowerPoint presentation, thinking that it shows value or at least hard work in preparation, but unless someone didn't expect you to work hard at all, printing the appendix looks like you are trying too hard. Instead, preparing for the Q&A and answering questions in a well though-out (in this case pre-thought out) manner will win you points in any investor meeting.

Bonus Slide Deck

Congratulations! You finished writing or at least planning how to write your first business plan! Now, even though investors and loan officers will expect a business plan, between us, they likely will skim through it or they might ask you to come and present your business idea and plan to them. Not a problem.

> *Take-away: The slide deck is just a series of slides covering the highlights of your business plan in powerful imagery!*

Depending on how much time you have, you can skip some slides during a presentation since each slide should stand by itself. It is organized this way so that there is a take home point in each slide without wasting the audience's time.

The slide deck can also be saved as a PDF and emailed ahead of time.

This is a simplified format for a slide deck. Each slide can be broken up into an additional 2-5 slides as long as each has a take home point in it. The elevator pitch is a 30 second pitch (2-3 lines of text) that explains the problem and the solution you have discovered. The market demographics expands on how big this problem is, followed by a more detailed explanation of the actual solution. Then the next few slides are how you are going to make money despite competition. What is the business model or strategy?

Then you end with a closer slide that is supposed to be your wow factor. Don't end with a 'thank you for your patience, any questions?' type of slide. You are not getting a pat on the back. Instead you are trying to get people to buy into your vision. There are entire books devoted to the slide deck, but you don't need to read them. Just remember the following points and practice will make your pitch sound perfect:

- **6 or fewer words per slide.** If you are trying to talk about financials or something complicated, then break it up into 3-4 points each with its own slide. Keep the irrelevant or the minor points in the appendix.

- **Lead with images and not text.** You want the audience to get an emotional response from your images so that they can agree with your slide even before you repeat the finding. If done correctly, the audience member should be nodding before or while you are explaining the slide.

- **Team Expertise.** If your team are experts in the field you are trying to build a business in, then start out with describing the Team <u>first</u> because the audience will give more weight to your words. In general, this is how salespeople start pitches by telling you how big the company is and how many clients it has in order to establish <u>credibility</u> before asking you to buy their product. On the other hand, if the team are amateurs without relevant experience, then keep the team pictures and bio in the end, because the audience will stop listening pretty quickly.

- **Practice the Q&A.** The audience has both experienced and inexperienced people in it. The experienced person will yawn and look away until they see something they haven't heard before or are skeptical. They then stay fixated on that thought until they can ask you after your presentation and those are usually the hard questions to answer, so practice! The inexperienced will miss out on what you were intending to say and then ask you to essentially simplify what you just said by applying it to a different market or a different situation. For example, you might be selling a spray paint to decorate your pet dog with your team's colors. The inexperienced audience member then asks you if that spray would work on cats.

Don't answer yes! The audience is asking you to explain again what it is you are selling. This is a good opportunity to expand on your product description and talk about how safe your product is.

Lastly, some food for thought when things go wrong. If one of the investors or audience members is aggressive during your pitch event, never ever become aggressive yourself or argue with the audience.

You've lost that investor and it may be because of your product or because of the way you were dressed. It doesn't matter. To salvage the situation in front of the other investors, just thank them for the (negative) input and answer only if they asked you a question. The minute you seem hostile or defensive, everyone in the room gets a red flag and they think to themselves 'life is too short to work with a-holes' even though you're probably a perfectly nice person.

Because people are generally risk-averse, they are not looking for a single reason to invest in you, they are rather looking for a single reason *not* to invest, and when they can't find one they say these musical words for any entrepreneur's ears "I can't find a single thing wrong with the business". Ah wouldn't that be nice? In reality, investors are bit more cautious and they end up investing in *tranches* (French for *slice*, and often used in relation to cake/pastry products). Thus, you'll get a tranche of the investment as you complete different milestones.

Final Thoughts

Having Completed this process and learned a few things along the way, we hope you enjoyed it. Here is how your business plan will eventually be organized:

Cover	Table of Contents	Executive Summary (Include Mission Statement and Summary)

Company Description (Not the **why** but the **what** of what you are selling)	Market Analysis (Demographics, STP, SWOT, Porter, PESTEL)	Organization & Management (Structure, Management, Board Members)
Product or Service (Description, Life Cycle, Competitive Advantage)	**Marketing & Sales Strategy** (Marking Mix [7Ps], Marketing Strategy, Sales Strategy)	**Financials** (Income Statement, Balance Sheet, Cashflow Statement highlights and/or summary)

Summary & Funding Required	**Appendix** (all pictures, figures,& tables, including your excel financial statements)	--Intentionally Left Blank--

One last final reminder! The business plan is a living document. You can change it at any point, especially when you have new information! Don't let someone tell you there is a specific length for any of the sections. It should be short enough to keep your audience's attention but long enough to be descriptive.

Hopefully you've learned something new and good luck drafting your business plan!

Be sure to check our other titles for a quick knowledge morsel.

How To
Incorporate
Your
Business